omans to Jude
Precise Christian Scripture Revealed

A How-To Guide for Unveiling Authentic Gospel Truth

Del Aaronson Publishing

Published by Del Aaronson Publishing, Whittier, CA

Printed in the United States of America
Cover design and book layout by Daniel Barrozo at the Ink Studio

Romans to Jude – Precise Christian Scripture Revealed

ISBN 978-0-615-40041-9
Library of Congress Control Number: 2010936280

Table of Contents

Introduction

"Long before there was ever a King James Version of our Bible, there was a gospel truth...and long before doctrines and denominations, the preeminence of the gospel was already ripe to harvest. Before man had ever thought about creating symbols to represent spiritual things...there was a gospel."
– C. White 2010

The gospel of Jesus Christ is often taught as the one infallible truth in America and across the globe. Our preachers preach it; our culture breeds it. We adhere to doctrines, embrace rituals and consider symbolic literature sacred. Whether born into or born again under the banner of Christianity, what has been presented to you and me as the "gospel truth" by churches, treatment programs, television ministries and books *is not the ultimate illustration of the gospel of Jesus Christ.* Believe it or not, there has *always* been something missing from every presentation of the greatest story ever told.

Right up front, let me say that neither time nor space will allow me to show you what's been missing, but I can surely point you in the right direction so you can gain these unique Biblical insights for yourself. In fact, if I were to show you what has been missing, I would only be repeating the same offense that so many others before me have committed: I would be defining the gospel *for you* according to my own doctrinal beliefs. I refuse to do this because the scriptures belong to you just as much as they do to me. Instead, what I'm offering here is a *dynamic reading strategy* that will help you realize the greater excellence of the gospel for yourself.

Some have questioned why I won't provide a defining commentary on each epistle that resides between Romans and Jude. My answer: yet another commentary is not what the average Christian needs. What is needed is an *unobstructed* view of the text; one that is not over-laid with the pretenses of men. On another front, the average Christian needs clear instruction on *how* to read the King James Version of the New Testament, especially Romans through Jude, because without an understanding of these specific scriptures, Christians will never truly understand the real relationship between the

Old and New Testaments nor will they truly and completely understand Matthew, Mark, Luke, John, Acts or Revelation in their truest light. It's a sad fact: most of us were never taught how to read the Bible correctly. Instead, we were trained to rely on an external authority for a ration of its contents. If you apply yourself in the way I suggest here, I promise that over time, the scriptures of the New Testament will spring to life like never before and you will be able to make greater sense of your Bible.

I will not be using this platform to overcome your idea of Romans through Jude with *my* interpretation of scripture, nor will I attempt to discourage you from following what you feel is right for you. What I propose here is to simply throw open the door of the gospel text wider than it has ever been opened in modern times, while at the same time, pointing you toward a more accurate revelation of what the gospel of Jesus Christ really is. I challenge you to dive into the New Testament deeper than you ever have, reading closely, allowing the wisdom of your inner man to have its say. Do this and the truth that you have been seeking will finally make its appearance right before your very own eyes.

A Fresh Look

$\mathcal{T}$aking *A Fresh Look* at the New Testament (Romans through Jude - KJV) requires that you do more than browse the text for the sheer purpose of substantiating and reinforcing the doctrines of your youth. This level of inquiry demands that you begin opening up to a greater revelation by asking the right questions, looking for the right answers, understanding the various answers, and then deciding what is in reality being communicated through the text. As soon as that which has been veiled by doctrine comes into full view, you will begin seeing the revelation of Christ for what it truly is—understanding that it has, and will always be, altogether too magnificent for a single religious group, doctrine or socio-political machine to claim only for itself. But discovering and experiencing the Truth anew in the ways I will be suggesting may be impossible until the gospel text is properly understood and pieced together without preconceived error. If we can understand the gospel text within its *intended context*, many series of readings (beginning with Romans and ending with Jude) will reveal what is absolute about the gospel while correcting inaccurate ideas that have been told to you in the past.

This may come as a shock, but here it is: the gospel of Jesus Christ, which most of us have been introduced to, has fallen far short of its original intent and purpose. I'm saddened to have to say this because it should never have happened. I'm *not* saying, in any way, that the gospel *itself* is flawed. What I am saying is this: Many of the gospel concepts that we've been taught have been erroneous illustrations of the full gospel. Instead of being made fully aware of the true mystery of Christ, we've been forced to drink watered down versions of the New Testament which have been taken completely out of context, misinterpreted, and then communicated as perfect truths. Throughout history religious leaders and teachers have, for whatever reasons (political, social or economic), *refused to deliver an unadulterated interpretation of the gospel.* The same kind of perversion continues today and is weakening the minds of well-meaning Christians the world over. It has to stop or Christians will continue to live lives that are saturated with *unbelief*, superstition and religious extremism. In 2011, Christians are still reading the King James version of Romans to Jude unskillfully, without any real command of its Old English prose or its allegory. Your misunderstanding is not your fault. We were all taught how to interpret what's there and what is or isn't between the lines, so that our present understanding would jive with someone else's incorrect interpretation of the gospel. The Truth has been co-opted, spun and in many instances utterly obliterated.

My mission for this study aid is simply to inspire all Bible-believing people to read and become more adept at truly understanding the width and depth of the gospel. What you've been led to believe about the gospel is strictly other peoples' basic *definition* of it. The gospel will forever be far more excellent than humankind's doctrines have reported it to be. The only way to see this reality for yourself is to assess the gospel texts *with your own eyes*.

While many people across time have presented long-established interpretations of the New Testament, no one has yet shared **how** to read the New Testament. In this study, I will. Romans through Jude begs to be looked upon with an intuitive eye—one that can see beyond the traditions of men and one that can embrace a truth independent of dual reasoning.

But how can this level of *seeing* occur if we've all been led to incorrect inferences and wrong conclusions? To understand the fullness of the gospel *exactly as it has been recorded in the text*—it's imperative that you begin reading your Bible with a direct perception of truth. With *Romans to Jude – Precise Christian Scripture Revealed* you'll begin the journey! And make no mistake: future generations are counting on us to ***get it right this time!***

Romans to Jude

*Y*ou may already have wondered, "*Why such emphasis on the twenty-one epistles that lie between Romans and Jude?*" For starters, this section of the Bible reveals the mystery of the gospel *in its fullness*. But to the untrained mind, the symbolic terms and allegory within these texts are easily ill-defined. However, for those who become skilled at extracting the less-obvious truths from the text, there is a vast storehouse of eye-opening revelations waiting to be uncovered and embraced.

To gain a real understanding of the texts in view, Romans through Jude must be read book-by-book, chapter-by-chapter and verse-by-verse—*with nothing taken out of context*. If you fail at this task—reading and interpreting the text correctly—you will also fail to recognize the less-obvious allegorical suggestions the writers use to refer to the truest nature of the gospel. Please understand: I'm not here to pass judgment or to challenge you on what you know or do not know about the gospel. I'm here simply to offer a reading strategy that will help you achieve a greater understanding of the gospel text for yourself. It will be your own depth of comprehension and degree of revelation which will propel you forward, not mine...*and that is as it should be.*

To completely understand the texts, one must evolve *beyond* the world of appearances to arrive at a place of single-mindedness, where love overcomes all unbelief. However, know that unless you have acquired a deeper knowledge of gospel terminology and inclined your ear to *His will*, what I've just said can in no way be interpreted correctly. These few words can be misinterpreted to mean something very different from what I intended to convey—and herein lies the problem: *The gospel of Jesus Christ, as revealed in the King James Bible, has not always been presented or understood perfectly in accordance with the glorious intent of its writers.* The misinterpretation and misuse of Biblical allegory has distorted and transformed the *intended* messages of the scriptures into man-made laws, falsehoods and socio-political stratagems. This has in fact retarded America's spiritual growth greatly and this is why I feel compelled to focus this study on Romans through Jude in the hope that we all might begin to increase in understanding, so that we may learn to live *according* to the gospel truth that is not only described in our Bibles, but innately written upon our very own souls.

Close Reading

$\mathcal{T}$o gain a greater understanding of the King James version of the New Testament, you will have to read it closely *many times*. I recommend that students with a Christian background begin their study with an intense focus on every epistle nestled between Romans and Jude. Do this book-by-book, chapter-by-chapter and verse-by-verse—because if you do, you will be properly prepared to receive the gospel message *in its fullness*—without fluff, delusion, or misinterpretation.

Close reading isn't a skill that can be developed to a high level of proficiency overnight, especially when tackling the King James version of the Bible, so take it slowly. As you learn how to do it properly (I'll show you how later on in this study), you will discover that close readings gracefully reveal the high purpose and sure applicability of the gospel. And although Old English may be a bit of a challenge for you, your maturing mind will, as you go along, gradually piece this glorious translation together properly over time. It will take months, possibly years of textual inquiry to master the discipline but if renewing your mind to the true gospel is your desire and is ever to occur, it will start right here, right now. The old days and ways of excerpting verses and pilfering passages out of context in an effort to communicate the gospel of Jesus Christ has surely run its course. The time has come for the *believer* to take full responsibility and *rise above* every faulty demonstration of the gospel truth. The text begs to be seen for what it truly is—an unadulterated view into the nature of the gospel of Jesus Christ.

✦ The Holy Bible is found in 80-90% of American homes. It is the most widely-published book in the world, and the least well understood. **_Why?_** In answering this question, first I would argue that it's because the gospel text has yet to be presented or understood in its entirety, having its special relationships of symbols properly discerned and communicated. Second, most Christians don't read their Bibles for themselves. Third, the doctrines of men still have preeminence in 2011 just as they did in 1611. Throughout history, religious orders and authorities have presented, dictated and shrouded what Christians are supposed to believe or not believe as their truth. I'm on a mission to help change these facts, and for this purpose I've prepared this study aid specifically for Christians and avid Bible readers who want to lay hold of an un-perverted version of the gospel—one that has not been watered down and whose light shines unobstructed. I have not come to bring you the latest *word from the Lord*, nor am I aiming to cater to any selfish desires, (wanna be rich, wanna control, wanna let ego rule.) Instead, I'm here to share a reading strategy that's specifically designed to take away all that prevents you from discerning and living the gospel as you ought. My plan is to escort you beyond the veil, to show you *how* to read with true accuracy and mature into what we've all been called to—the mind of Christ.

Gospel Mathematics

$\mathcal{M}$astering the gospel text is similar to mastering the principles of mathematics. First you learn the basics—addition, subtraction, multiplication and division. Then comes algebra where you learn to deal with relationships, representations, specifics and systems. I consider these two disciplines to be comparable in that mathematics is the science of numbers and their operations just as the gospel is the knowledge of transcendent truth and its application. If we ever hope to develop our spiritual minds to greater complexity and depth, mastering basic principles is required. Without it, you and I can only hope to be guided by guesswork, not by principle. Consequently, guesswork can only produce false doctrine—and where there is false doctrine, there is incorrect teaching—and where there is incorrect teaching there is a lack of understanding—and where there is a lack of understanding, *oneness* (which is the goal of the gospel) in Christ can never be achieved. It's impossible for us to understand the miracles and *works* of *Christ* before we've completely understood the principles of *Christ*—and unless the principles of *Christ* are understood, one cannot *know Christ*—and if one does not *know Christ* then one cannot authentically *preach Christ* and do that which is *perfect and good*.

As Christian seekers, we'll always be kept from entering into the depths of the gospel until each of us has earned our own right to graduate into the holy of holies. But how can we prepare ourselves for graduation without receiving (through self effort) an accurate presentation or revelation of the gospel? Moreover, what happens to those of us who do not take responsibility to discover the innate gospel for ourselves? If we continue waiting on someone else to teach us the gospel, how will we ever come face-to-face with what Ephesians describes as the mystery of Christ? How can it ever be obtained unless we seek it for ourselves?

Gospel Terminology

$\mathcal{G}$aining an accurate sense of gospel texts requires New Testament students to learn its terminology and the special system of relationships each of the words has within the text. Readers must have a sure, complete understanding of each symbolic piece of language used by the gospel writers. When terminology and symbols are rightly discerned and understood, your initiation into the oracles of God begins and the wondrous reality of liberty unveils itself to you. A *mature* knowledge of gospel terminology will quickly separate you from all old wives' fables, church clichés, superstition, and self-righteous dogma. This is the place where the perfect knowledge of Christ begins to peek through the veil of tradition and inspire the heart to apprehend that which it was called to obtain.

Remember: Gaining perfect knowledge of the gospel through its terms and symbols is a labor-intense process and will take considerable time and study to acquire, but if you'll embrace the process as a labor of love, it won't hurt much at all. You simply can't examine Romans through Jude in a certain number of readings. It has taken me sixteen years of reading and re-reading to see into the text the way I do now. Over the years I've been able to dispel many myths and expose many erroneous teachings that have emanated from the mouths and pens of men. Trust me. If you take the same opportunity to read the text for yourself, you too will be amazed at what Romans through Jude actually teaches.

During this process you may often find yourself wondering why the gospel was never presented with as much clarity as you are suddenly beginning to receive. You might even become irritated and begin questioning the origins and validity of your own Christian experience. Mastering Romans through Jude isn't easy. You must read the text correctly and understand its allegorical elements or you'll remain estranged from what the original writers labored so faithfully to prove to you.

In this study aid I've included next 123 *must know* words found in Romans through Jude. Your first assignment is to self-administer a mock vocabulary quiz using this list. Without using a dictionary, write down your own personal definition of each word. When you're finished, simply fold your sheets of paper in half and tuck them between the pages of this book. Right now, the rightness or wrongness of your definitions isn't all that important, because the purpose of the exercise is to help you *measure your current knowledge of gospel terms against your future knowledge of these same words*. An accurate understanding of scripture is what we're after, so I can quickly assure you that your close readings will reveal far more than you already know with regard to these words. The most important thing is to allow a greater perspective of the gospel to make its way into your heart and mind. In time, you'll see the New Testament much more clearly...I promise.

123 MUST KNOW WORDS

Abraham	Abundant	Adam	Adultery
Allegory	Angel	Anti-Christ	Apostleship
Ask	Baptism	Belief	Believer
Blood	Bond	Born again	Born of
Christ	Circumcision	Circumspect	Darkness
Death	Deed	Devil	Devilish
Discernment	Disobedience	Divorce	Doctrine
Evil	Faith	Faithful	False prophet
First born	Forgiveness	Fornication	Gift
Glory	Good	Gospel	Grace
Greek	Heart	Heaven	Holiness
Hope	Humble	Idolatry	Image
Inheritance	Jew	Jesus Christ	Joy

Judgment	Kingdom	Labor	Liberty
Light	Love	Lust	Marriage
Meat	Melchisedec	Mercy	Milk
Mind	Minister	Mystery	New Testament
Obedience	Old Testament	Overcome	Partaker
Patience	Peace	Perfection	Prayer
Preach	Promise	Rejoice	Religion
Repentance	Resurrection	Rest	Revelation
Righteousness	Risen	Saints	Salvation
Sanctification	Satan	Saved	Seed
Sensual	Servant	Sin	Singleness
Son of God	Spirit of error	Spirit of truth	Sufferings
Supply	Symbolism	Temple	Thanksgiving
The Cross	The World	Things	Tradition
Trespasses	Truth	Unbelief	Uncircumcision
Unrighteousness	Vanity	Veil	Wicked
Will of God	Wisdom	Witchcraft	Wives' fables
Works	Worship	Wrong	

After going through this list, I figure that you might expect me to provide you with the same definitions that tradition had led us all to believe. *Fortunately for you*, I will not. Life experience has shown me that a deep understanding of God comes only by revelation—and it is in the interest of your own revelation that I dare not hinder you from receiving clarity in your own time through your own efforts. For even the Apostle Paul did not learn the gospel from any man, but obtained his knowledge by revelation.

With time, you will become very familiar with how and why the writers of the gospel used certain terms and contrasts to describe the promise and calling of God. You'll also find that you are reaching beyond the boundaries of doctrine and every other incorrect concept of the gospel that has ever come your way. Your increasingly-accurate understanding of these terms will allow you to see that what you've heard and accepted in the past concerning the gospel is elementary in scope and *does not completely line up* with the highest of intentions recorded throughout the New Testament. This guide is your opportunity to experience *your* truth—a truth that transcends all doctrine, all man-made laws and all traditions—not according to my definitions or those of other men, but by the definitions revealed to you by the Spirit of God.

The Notion of Two Thoughts

$\mathscr{A}$nother vital terminology exercise that's on your to-do list within these pages is what I call the **Notion of Two Thoughts**. In this exercise, you will investigate the opposite nature of fifty-two key gospel terms. Again, with reading practice, the truths of these contrasts will make themselves available to you and you will be well on your way to "getting" exactly what the original writers intended for you to understand. Please remember: each epistle between Romans and Jude must be read chapter-by-chapter and verse-by-verse, otherwise these fifty-two terms (and the previous 123 terms) will not come alive to you as they ought. Please: Never take shortcuts that call for scripture excerpting. An abbreviated strategy will never give you the full right to enter into the depths of the gospel. Upon realizing the highest intentions of the text, the less-obvious becomes very obvious indeed and your understanding of gospel truth will begin to connect with all that is innate and indivisible within the gospel of Jesus Christ. Remember: accuracy and clarity are your goals. In time, you will see... Trust the process and take your time.

TWO THOUGHTS

Jews – Gentiles	Good – Evil
His will – Your will	Heaven – Earth
Male – Female	Old Testament – New Testament
Milk – Meat	Righteousness – Unrighteousness
Holy – Unholy	Love – Hate
Death – Resurrection	Corruptible – Incorruptible
Old man – New man	Work – Rest
Ascend – Descend	Godliness – Idolatry
Darkness – Light	Obedience – Disobedience
Wives – Husbands	Baptism – Risen
Doing wrong – Doing good	Fornication – Virginity
Adultery – Singleness	Law of the Mind – Law of the Spirit
Light – Darkness	Marriage – Divorce

Transitions and Conjunctions

$\mathcal{W}$hen taking on Romans through Jude it's important to understand the power of each transition and conjunction or you risk misinterpreting the text completely. An understanding of how these words work within the Old English prose of the New Testament is critically necessary for you to gain greater clarity.

Transitional words in the New Testament both *guide readers from one significant idea to the next* and *help readers understand the relationship between spiritual and earthly ideas.* These words act as signposts so readers can follow the writer's train of thought. Transition words are used to: compare two things, contrast two things, show time, emphasize a point, conclude or summarize, add information, and to clarify. Transitions tell a reader *what to do with the information the writer has presented* and *how to think about, organize, and react to old and new ideas.*

Conjunctions connect parts of a sentence. They can suggest chronological order, inclusiveness, contrast, affirmation, exception, restatement, and correction. They can also create complex relationships between ideas.

It's imperative that you go beyond the elementary (milk stage) in order to apprehend that which is excellent and mature (meat stage). To do this, respect and pay vivid attention to every transition and conjunction as you study, because *without acknowledging them* as guideposts along the way, your understanding of New Testament scripture will be limited and very inaccurate.

TRANSITIONS AND CONJUNCTIONS

In – used to indicate inclusion within something abstract or immaterial
But – unless; if not; except that; otherwise than
Is – equal to
Wherein – in which location; where/in what way; how
We – used to indicate a particular profession, nationality, political party, etc.
In whom – the objective case of Who
Unto/until – used for expressing motion or direction toward a point, person, place, or thing approached or reached
With – implying interaction, association, connection
And – added to; then again;
Whereby – by or through which
Since – between a particular past time and the present
Thereupon – immediately following that

Were – existed as
Both – two together
What – to indicate that which
By – through the agency, efficacy, work, participation, or authority of
Rather – more readily or willingly
Through – by the way or agency of
Therefore – as a result; consequently
Us – used to indicate a particular profession, nationality, political party, etc.
Who – of what character, origin, position, importance, etc.
Which – being previously mentioned
Even – to emphasize occurrence, coincidence or simultaneousness of occurrences
According – to cause to conform or agree; bring into harmony
Henceforth – from now on; from this point forward
Then – immediately or soon after
Before – ahead of, in advance of
Are – to be
Or – otherwise
Howbeit – nevertheless
Be – to exist or live
Of – used to indicate possession, connection or association
Therein – in that place, time or thing
One – of the same, having a single kind, nature or condition
Yet – in addition; again
It – used to represent a concept or abstract idea understood or previously stated
That – implies a contrast or contradistinction
Neither – not the one or the other
If – on the condition that
After – in agreement or in unison with
For – in place of; instead of
Hitherto – until now
Moreover – in addition to what has been said
Likewise – also; too
Nevertheless – in spite of that; however
Thereof – of or concerning this

Reading Instructions

*I*tems you will need:

a. King James Version of the New Testament

b. Dictionary

c. Ink pen

d. Highlighter

*R*eading Instructions:

1. Read the complete book of Romans beginning at chapter one, verse one. Read the text at your usual, normal speed. While circling, underlining and highlighting words found on the gospel terminology list on pages 21 and 22 of this book, please mark any additional words or phrases that command your attention, especially any that are unfamiliar. Keep your

dictionary handy; some of the words not on our list may require actual real-world definitions. As you read over groups of verses, look for items that may also qualify as main ideas. Main ideas will, at some point, qualify as *unifying principles within chapters* and will keep you on target to proving the scriptures. Understanding the gospel by way of allegorical interpretation is not easy. It is a real process and doesn't happen overnight, so don't stress over it. (Besides, during your first few readings you'll be only familiarizing yourself with the language patterns of the Old English prose.) The more you read, the more you'll find—and over time you'll get better at arranging, defining and mastering the unique set of vocabulary words found in each epistle of the New Testament.

2. Next, move on to 1st Corinthians and repeat step one. Do the same with the remaining nineteen books, 2nd Corinthians through Jude.

Whether it takes three weeks or three months to complete steps 1 and 2, you're now ready to revisit the texts again, beginning with Romans, the first chapter and first verse. This time through, read more slowly and carefully. You should again come across a few items that commanded your attention during the first read through. Keep them in mind and begin re-reading with the intention of building upon the items that sparked your curiosity. Continue marking terms and phrases that are significant to you. I encourage you also to mark transitions and conjunctions while remembering that they are vivid, special guideposts that point you rightly toward additional light and comprehension. As time goes on you'll become more conscious of each contrasting element of language hidden within the text. Mark these connections and relationships as you spot them. Marking contrasting elements and analyzing them in context will prove just how inadequate excerpting scripture can be, and it will also set fire to the innate, ushering you into a more certain and accurate gospel truth.

During subsequent readings please make a conscious attempt to isolate the most important generalizations within each chapter of each book. Do your best to follow the writer's line of thought and open yourself to his main point. Begin asking: WHAT is the author trying to prove? WHAT is the unifying principle of each chapter? WHAT idea does the collection of verses in each chapter refer to? Soon, you'll discover that the writers don't state their entire idea about the gospel within the brevity of a verse, or even a chapter, but they will however give you a piece of the idea a little bit at a time...As your reading continues, the fullness will become obvious across time. Occasionally, you'll find verses and groups of verses that don't seem to accomplish much. For example, some groups of verses are purely illustrative; others may be comments or mere impressions by the writer. Just remember to keep your eye on *the unifying principle* throughout each chapter.

A word of advice: Please don't get preoccupied with the historical, social or political ideas that are scattered throughout the text. What was viewed hundreds of years ago as correct or incorrect to a certain culture, political faction or religious power will probably carry little relevance in today's multicultural society. I understand that many can and will argue this point, but my aim here is not to argue historical, social or political stances, past or present: my sole aim is to share a reading strategy that's designed to take you *beyond* the limits of theology and doctrine. This book is not aimed at changing your religion; it was written to challenge you to read your own Bible so you can, once and for all, prove to yourself what is correct and accurate regarding the full gospel of Jesus Christ.

To view my actual text markings in the first chapter of Ephesians, please see Figures 1A and 1B on pages 77 and 78.

The Strategy of WHAT

*T*he Strategy of WHAT is a reading strategy designed to unlock and extract less-obvious intentions from the pages of the New Testament. While simple to apply, it can't function as designed unless you, as a Bible reader, can connect intuitively with the technique. In addition to marking the text, you will also need to ask certain questions about each verse. Each question must be aimed at finding out WHAT, WHO, HOW and ACCORDING TO WHAT. This is the time to listen (intuitively within) for the right answers, understand the answers, and then decide what the original writers have truly communicated to you. This unique approach will prepare your mind for a level of truth that has not been revealed to you through traditional Christian theology and doctrine. If approached correctly, these questions will unearth truths that have been right under our noses for hundreds, if not thousands of years. Let's take a look at Romans, chapter one, verse one to see exactly how the Strategy of WHAT should be applied:

> *Paul, a servant of Jesus Christ, called to be an apostle, separated unto the gospel of God...*

Looking at verse one, is there any word, term or phrase that needs to be asked WHAT it is, WHO it is, or HOW it is? Please examine the following list of WHAT questions that I personally extracted from verse one to see just how easy this can be:

a. **What is a servant?**
b. **What/Who is Jesus Christ?**
c. **What is a servant of Christ?**
d. **What does it mean to be called?**
e. **What is an apostle?**
f. **What does it mean to be called to be an apostle?**
g. **What is the gospel?**
h. **What does it mean to be separated unto the gospel of God?**
i. **What is the gospel of God?**

Did you ever dream there could be so many questions to ask about a single Bible verse? At one time, neither did I! Make the effort to question the text in this manner and I promise that in time you'll find yourself walking in much greater understanding of the gospel. Asking WHAT questions may be the easiest part of this strategy; answering the questions *accurately* will be the greater challenge. Failure to correctly answer any of the questions will derail your study. You need to discern the answers in order to recognize all that awaits you beyond the walls of common gospel rhetoric.

Take a look back at the questions I posed. Consider each of the nine WHAT questions I asked with regard to verse one. At first glance, you may think you know the answers, but remember, whatever you're thinking may well be elementary in scope and ultimately inaccurate according to what the original writers were expecting to share. Unless you've previously gone through the process of reading and re-reading Romans through Jude tens of times while mastering the gospel text, you have little to draw from except the doctrines that you've been exposed to. This is why I can suggest (even argue) that your preliminary answers to these WHAT questions will almost certainly be inaccurate. Until you've become expertly acquainted with a verse's flow of prose and allegory for yourself, the New Testament will always be defined through the eyes of someone else's theology and doctrine. This is why you must read the Bible for yourselves—so you come face to face with its unadulterated truth. Simply follow the example I've set forth above. I guarantee that the Strategy of WHAT will make an incredible difference in the way you process the gospel truth in your heart and mind.

There is no real secret to answering WHAT questions except that you must "give it time" and adhere to the following:

1. Read, re-read and read again Romans through Jude, book-by-book, chapter-by-chapter and verse–by-verse.
2. DO NOT skip around, excerpt or take passages out of context.
3. Read through an entire chapter before making any judgments.
4. Define all gospel terms and allegories with pinpoint accuracy.
5. Listen for the right answers and then decide what the writers are truly saying.

As an example, I have applied the Strategy of WHAT to the entire first three chapters of Romans for you. You can find them after the conclusion to this study aid. Please take the time to apply the strategy to all subsequent chapters and books after you've read them—remembering to ask WHAT, WHO, HOW and ACCORDING TO WHAT. Over time as your close reading and text marking continues the answers to your WHAT questions will begin appearing as pieces to a puzzle. You may have to read Romans through Jude in its entirety an untold number of times before the pieces begin to reveal themselves, but eventually they will. In most cases the pieces will come from entirely different chapters and books, but the more you read and re-read, the more these remembered pieces will remind you of their existence elsewhere. There will be no need to dig for the answers…they will simply rise to the surfaces of the pages the more and more you read. Please don't put any time constraints on the process. Soon enough you will have command of the gospel text like never before and will come to know the nature of the gospel of Christ for yourself.

The Strategy of WHAT Study Guides are available in eBook form at www.RomansToJude.com/studyguide

Conclusion

$\mathcal{F}$riends, I hope I've been of considerable help to you—a small spark of inspiration to encourage you to seek out your truth as never before. I sincerely hope that, from this point forward, you'll allow the gospel text to show you what and who *Christ* truly is. What *belief* and *unbelief* is. What *sin* is. What the *devil* is. What *repentance* is. What *reconciliation* is. What *humility* is. What *prayer* is. What *hope* is. What the *cross* is. What *death* is. What *baptism* is. What *worship* is. What *work* is. What *labor* is. What *adultery* is and what the *glory* of God is. For without an evolved level of insight, the gospel has no choice but to remain hidden in an elementary state, veiled by theology and doctrine. Please understand: you have a God-given **right**

45

to *know* the fullness of Christ for yourself—without limitation and without distraction.

Short of providing definitions and answers for you, I hope I have at least challenged you to reach for more of the *meat* rather than more of the same old *milk by-product*. Truthfully, it will be very difficult for you to fully understand the miracles and *works* of *Christ* until you understand the principles of *Christ*. Because unless the *principles* of *Christ* are understood, you will never come to fully *know Christ* —and if you are unable to fully *know Christ* you'll be forever unable to authentically *preach Christ and will* forfeit your opportunity to do that which is *good* and *perfect*. So, please…try my approach. Question the Biblical text Romans through Jude like never before—ask repeatedly until you, yourself, become a master of Christian literature and a bona fide steward of the mystery. Take a fresh look *now*. The unobstructed light will cause you to finally see with clarity…I promise.

Strategy of WHAT Applied
ROMANS – SAMPLE CHAPTER 1

All 21 Strategy of WHAT Study Guides are Available at RomansToJude.com/studyguide

¹*Paul, a servant of Jesus Christ, called to be an apostle, separated unto the gospel of God,*
a. What is a servant?
b. What/Who is Jesus Christ?
c. What is a servant of Christ?
d. What does it mean to be called?
e. What is an apostle?
f. What does it mean to be called to be an apostle?
g. What is the gospel?
h. What does it mean to be separated unto the gospel of God?
i. What is the gospel of God?

²*(Which he had promised afore by his prophets in the holy scriptures,)*
a. Who is he?

b.   What had he promised afore?

c.   What is a prophet?

d.   What are holy scriptures?

e.   What is holiness?

³*Concerning his Son Jesus Christ our Lord, which was made of the seed of David according to the flesh;*

a.   What/Who did the promise concern?

b.   What is the Lord?

c.   What/Who is Christ our Lord?

d.   What is the seed?

e.   What is the seed of David?

f.   How was Christ made of the seed of David?

⁴*And declared to be the Son of God with power, according to the spirit of holiness, by the resurrection from the dead:*

a.   What/Who is the Son of God?

b.   What is a son of God?

c.   How can one be declared to be the Son of God with power?

d.   What is power?

e.   What is the spirit of holiness?

f.   What is holiness?

g.   What is according to the spirit of holiness?

h.   What is the resurrection from the dead?

i.   What does it mean to be dead?

⁵*By whom we have received grace and apostleship, for obedience to the faith among all nations, for his name:*

a.   What is grace?

b.   How can one receive grace?

c. What is apostleship?
d. What is obedience?
e. What is faith?
f. What does it mean to have obedience to the faith?
g. What does *his name* signify?

⁶*Among whom are ye also the called of Jesus Christ:*
a. What/Who are the called?
b. What is Christ?
c. What does it mean to be the *called* of Jesus Christ?

⁷*To all that be in Rome, beloved of God, called to be saints: Grace to you and peace from God our Father, and the Lord Jesus Christ.*
a. What does it mean to be beloved of God?
b. What is a saint?
c. What does it mean to be *called* to be a saint?
d. What is grace?
e. What is peace?
f. What/Who is God?
g. What/Who is the Father?
h. What/Who is the Lord?
i. What is Christ?

⁸*First, I thank my God through Jesus Christ for you all, that your faith is spoken of throughout the whole world.*
a. Who did Paul thank first?
b. What is the significance of the writer referring to God as 'my God?'
c. How does one thank God through Christ?
d. What is faith?

e.   What is the world?

⁹For God is my witness, whom I serve with my spirit in the gospel of his Son, that without ceasing I make mention of you always in my prayers;

a.   What is a witness?

b.   How can God be a witness?

c.   What is the gospel?

d.   What is the gospel of his Son?

e.   How does Paul serve with his spirit *in* the gospel?

f.   How can one serve *in* the gospel without ceasing?

g.   What are prayers?

h.   What enabled Paul to pray without ceasing?

i.   How did Paul make mention in prayer?

¹⁰Making request, if by any means now at length I might have a prosperous journey by the will of God to come unto you.

a.   What does it mean to make request?

b.   What is the will of God?

c.   What is a prosperous journey by the will of God?

¹¹For I long to see you, that I may impart unto you some spiritual gift, to the end ye may be established;

a.   What is a spiritual gift?

b.   What is *the end*?

c.   How does one become established?

d.   What could Paul impart to establish those called to be saints?

¹²That is, that I may be comforted together with you by the mutual faith both of you and me.

a. What is faith?
b. What is mutual faith?
c. What is the purpose of Paul being comforted *together* with those called to be saints?

¹³*Now I would not have you ignorant, brethren, that oftentimes I purposed to come unto you, (but was let hitherto,) that I might have some fruit among you also, even as among other Gentiles.*
a. What is ignorance?
b. What is fruit?
c. What/Who are Gentiles?

¹⁴*I am debtor both to the Greeks, and to the Barbarians; both to the wise, and to the unwise.*
a. What/Who are Greeks/Barbarians?
b. What/Who are the wise?
c. What/Who are the unwise?
d. How can Paul be debtor to *both*?

¹⁵*So, as much as in me is, I am ready to preach the gospel to you that are at Rome also.*
a. What is the gospel?
b. What does it mean to preach?
c. How does the gospel get preached?

¹⁶*For I am not ashamed of the gospel of Christ: for it is the power of God unto salvation to every one that believeth; to the Jew first, and also to the Greek.*
a. What is Christ?
b. What is the gospel?

c. What is the gospel of Christ?
d. Why was Paul not ashamed of the gospel?
e. What does it mean to be ashamed of the gospel?
f. What is the power of God?
g. What is salvation?
h. How does the gospel of Christ lead to salvation?
i. What is belief?
j. What is a Jew?
k. Why did Paul mention that the Jew was first?
l. What/Who are the Greek and why are they after the Jew?
m. How is the power of God made available to everyone?
n. Who are they that believe?

[17] *For therein is the righteousness of God revealed from faith to faith: as it is written, The just shall live by faith.*
a. What is righteousness?
b. What is the righteousness of God?
c. Where is the righteousness of God revealed?
d. What is faith?
e. How is the righteousness of God revealed from faith to faith?
f. Who are the just?
g. What does it mean to live by faith?
h. How do the just live by faith?

[18] *For the wrath of God is revealed from heaven against all ungodliness and unrighteousness of men, who hold the truth in unrighteousness;*
a. What is wrath?
b. What is the wrath of God?
c. What is heaven?

d. How is the wrath of God revealed?
e. What is ungodliness?
f. What is unrighteousness?
g. What is the unrighteousness of men?
h. What is the truth?
i. How can the truth be held in unrighteousness?

[19]*Because that which may be known of God is manifest in them; for God hath shewed it unto them.*
a. What can be known of God?
b. What did God manifest in the just and the ungodly/ unrighteous?
c. What has God shown to the just and the ungodly/ unrighteous?

[20]*For the invisible things of him from the creation of the world are clearly seen, being understood by the things that are made, even his eternal power and Godhead; so that they are without excuse:*
a. What are invisible things?
b. What are the invisible things of him?
c. What is eternal power?
d. What is the Godhead?
e. Why are the ungodly/unrighteous without excuse?

[21]*Because that, when they knew God, they glorified him not as God, neither were thankful; but became vain in their imaginations, and their foolish heart was darkened.*
a. What does it mean to glorify God as God?
b. How can one show themselves thankful?
c. What were *their* imaginations?

d.   What does vanity have to do with the imagination?
e.   What is heart?
f.   What is a foolish heart?
g.   What did it mean to have *their* foolish heart darkened?

[22] *Professing themselves to be wise, they became fools,*

a.   How do the ungodly/unrighteous profess themselves to be wise?
b.   What is a fool?

[23] *And changed the glory of the uncorruptible God into an image made like to corruptible man, and to birds, and fourfooted beasts, and creeping things.*

a.   What is glory?
b.   What does it mean to be uncorruptible?
c.   What is the uncorruptible God?
d.   What is the glory of the uncorruptible God?
e.   How can fools change the glory of the uncorruptible God?
f.   What is an image?
g.   What is corruptible man?

[24] *Wherefore God also gave them up to uncleanness through the lusts of their own hearts, to dishonour their own bodies between themselves:*

a.   What is uncleanness?
b.   What is lust?
c.   What is the lust of a fool's heart?
d.   What does it mean that they *dishonored their own bodies between themselves*?

²⁵ *Who changed the truth of God into a lie, and worshipped and served the creature more than the Creator, who is blessed forever. Amen.*

a. What is the truth of God?
b. Who changed the truth of God into a lie?
c. What is worship?
d. What does it mean for one to serve the creature more than the Creator?
e. How the Creator be blessed forever?
f. What does Amen mean? What is its significance in this verse?

²⁶ *For this cause God gave them up unto vile affections: for even their women did change the natural use into that which is against nature:*

a. For what *cause*?
b. What are vile affections?
c. What does the word *women* signify?
d. How can the natural use of a *woman* be changed?
e. What does it mean to be *against* nature?

²⁷ *And likewise also the men, leaving the natural use of the woman, burned in their lust one toward another; men with men working that which is unseemly, and receiving in themselves that recompence of their error which was meet.*

a. What does it mean for a man to leave the natural use of a "woman?"
b. What is lust?
c. What are *men*?
d. How can a man burn is his lust towards other *men*?
e. What is unseemly?

f. What is recompense?
g. What is error?
h. What is the error of *men*?

²⁸*And even as they did not like to retain God in their knowledge, God gave them over to a reprobate mind, to do those things which are not convenient;*
a. Who are *they*?
b. What is knowledge?
c. What does it mean to retain God in one's knowledge?
d. What is a reprobate mind?
e. What are *those things*?
f. What is not convenient?
g. How can one do that which is not convenient?

²⁹*Being filled with all unrighteousness, fornication, wickedness, covetousness, maliciousness; full of envy, murder, debate, deceit, malignity; whisperers,*
a. What is unrighteousness?
b. What is fornication?
c. What is wickedness?
d. What is covetousness?
e. What is the connection between unrighteousness and *things* that are not convenient?

³⁰*Backbiters, haters of God, despiteful, proud, boasters, inventors of evil things, disobedient to parents,*
a. What is a hater of God?
b. What is evil?
c. What are evil things?

[31] *Without understanding, covenant breakers, without natural affection, implacable, unmerciful:*
a. What is *understanding*?
b. What does it mean to be without understanding?
c. What is a covenant?
d. What is natural affection?

[32] *Who knowing the judgment of God, that they which commit such things are worthy of death, not only do the same, but have pleasure in them that do them.*
a. What is judgment?
b. What is the judgment of God?
c. What does it mean to know the judgment of God?
d. What are *such things*?
e. What is death?
f. What does it mean to be worthy *this* death?
g. Who is worthy of *this* death?

ROMANS – SAMPLE CHAPTER 2

All 21 Strategy of WHAT Study Guides are Available at RomansToJude.com/studyguide

[1] *Therefore thou art inexcusable, O man, whosoever thou art that judgest: for wherein thou judgest another, thou condemnest thyself; for thou that judgest doest the same things.*
a. What is inexcusable?
b. What is judging?
c. What does it mean to judge another?
d. How can one condemn himself?

[2] But we are sure that the judgment of God is according to truth against them which commit such things.

a. What is the judgment of God?
b. What is truth?
c. How is the judgment of God according to truth?
d. Who is the judgment of God against?
e. What are *such things*?
f. Who are *them* who commit such things?

[3] And thinkest thou this, O man, that judgest them which do such things, and doest the same, that thou shalt escape the judgment of God?

a. What is the judgment of God?
b. Can the judgment of God be escaped?

[4] Or despisest thou the riches of his goodness and forbearance and longsuffering; not knowing that the goodness of God leadeth thee to repentance?

a. What are the riches of his goodness?
b. What is forbearance and longsuffering?
c. How can one despise his goodness and forbearance and longsuffering?
d. What is the goodness of God?
e. What is repentance?
f. How does the goodness of God lead to repentance?

[5] But after thy hardness and impenitent heart treasurest up unto thyself wrath against the day of wrath and revelation of the righteous judgment of God;

a. What is hardness?
b. What is an impenitent heart?

c. What does it mean to *treasurest up unto thyself?*
d. What is wrath?
e. What is revelation of the righteous judgment of God?

[6] *Who will render to every man according to his deeds:*
a. Who will render?
b. What are deeds?
c. Why is there a rendering to every man according to his deeds?

[7] *To them who by patient continuance in well doing seek for glory and honour and immortality, eternal life:*
a. Who are *them*?
b. What is well doing?
c. What is patient continuance?
d. What are glory, honour, immortality and eternal life?
e. How does one *seek* for glory, honour, immortality and eternal life?

[8] *But unto them that are contentious, and do not obey the truth, but obey unrighteousness, indignation and wrath,*
a. Who are *them*?
b. What does contentious mean?
c. What is the truth?
d. How can one not obey the truth?
e. What is unrighteousness, indignation and wrath?
f. What does it mean to obey unrighteousness?

[9] *Tribulation and anguish, upon every soul of man that doeth evil, of the Jew first, and also of the Gentile;*
a. What is tribulation?

b. What is anguish?
c. What is the soul of man?
d. What is evil?
e. What does it mean to *doeth* evil?
f. What is a Jew?
g. What is a Gentile?
h. Why is tribulation and anguish upon the Jew first?
i. Why is tribulation and anguish upon the Gentile also?

¹⁰*But glory, honour, and peace, to every man that worketh good, to the Jew first, and also to the Gentile:*
a. What is glory, honour and peace?
b. What is good?
c. How can one *worketh* good?
d. Why is glory, honour and peace to the Jew First?
e. What is a Jew?
f. Why is glory, honour and peace also to the Gentile?

¹¹*For there is no respect of persons with God.*
a. What is *respect of persons*?
b. Why is there no respect of persons with God?

¹²*For as many as have sinned without law shall also perish without law: and as many as have sinned in the law shall be judged by the law;*
a. What is sin?
b. What is law?
c. How can one sin *without* the law?
d. What does it mean to perish?
e. How can one perish *without* the law?

f.   How can one sin *in* the law?

g.   How does the law judge?

[13] *(For not the hearers of the law are just before God, but the doers of the law shall be justified.*

a.   What is the law?

b.   What is a hearer of the law?

c.   Who are the just?

d.   What does it mean to be *just* before God?

e.   What is a doer of the law?

f.   What does it mean to be justified?

g.   Why shall the doers of the law be justified?

[14] *For when the Gentiles, which have not the law, do by nature the things contained in the law, these, having not the law, are a law unto themselves:*

a.   What is a Gentile?

b.   Why are Gentiles without the law?

c.   What do Gentiles do by nature?

d.   What is the law?

e.   What are the *things* contained in the law?

f.   How can the Gentiles be a law unto themselves?

[15] *Which shew the work of the law written in their hearts, their conscience also bearing witness, and their thoughts the mean while accusing or else excusing one another;)*

a.   What is the work of the law?

b.   Who shew the work of the law written in their hearts?

c.   How can the conscience bear witness?

d.   How do the thoughts bear witness?

[16]*In the day when God shall judge the secrets of men by Jesus Christ according to my gospel.*
a. How does God judge?
b. What are the secrets of men?
c. What does it mean for God to judge *by* Jesus Christ?
d. What is the gospel?

[17]*Behold, thou art called a Jew, and restest in the law, and makest thy boast of God,*
a. What is a Jew?
b. What is the law?
c. What does it mean to *rest* in the law?
d. How can a Jew rest in the law and make his boast of God?

[18]*And knowest his will, and approvest the things that are more excellent, being instructed out of the law;*
a. What is *his* will?
b. Why can Jews *know* his will?
c. What *things* are more excellent?
d. What is the law?

[19]*And art confident that thou thyself art a guide of the blind, a light of them which are in darkness,*
a. What does it mean to be blind?
b. Who are the blind?
c. What does it mean to be in darkness?
d. Who are *them* which are in darkness?
e. Why is a Jew confident that he is a guide of the blind?

[20]*An instructor of the foolish, a teacher of babes, which hast the form of knowledge and of the truth in the law.*

a. Who are the foolish?
b. Who are the babes?
c. What is a babe?
d. What is the *form* of knowledge?
e. What is the *form* of the truth?
f. What is the truth *in* the law?

[21] *Thou therefore which teachest another, teachest thou not thyself? Thou that preachest a man should not steal, dost thou steal?*
a. What is teaching?
b. What is preaching?

[22] *Thou that sayest a man should not commit adultery, dost thou commit adultery? thou that abhorrest idols, dost thou commit sacrilege?*
a. Who is *thou* that sayest?
b. What is adultery?
c. Why should a man not commit adultery?
d. What are idols?
e. What is sacrilege?

[23] *Thou that makest thy boast of the law, through breaking the law dishonourest thou God?*
a. What is the law?
b. How is God dishonored?

[24] *For the name of God is blasphemed among the Gentiles through you, as it is written.*
a. What is the *name* of God?
b. How is the name of God blasphemed among the Gentiles?

c.   Who blasphemed the name of God among the Gentiles?

²⁵ *For circumcision verily profiteth, if thou keep the law: but if thou be a breaker of the law, thy circumcision is made uncircumcision.*
a.   What is circumcision?
b.   How does one keep the law?
c.   How does one break the law?
d.   What is uncircumcision?

²⁶ *Therefore if the uncircumcision keep the righteousness of the law, shall not his uncircumcision be counted for circumcision?*
a.   Who are the uncircumcision?
b.   What is righteousness?
c.   What is the righteousness of the law?
d.   How can one keep the righteousness of the law?
e.   How can uncircumcision be counted for circumcision?

²⁷ *And shall not uncircumcision which is by nature, if it fulfil the law, judge thee, who by the letter and circumcision dost transgress the law?*
a.   What is the uncircumcision which is *by* nature?
b.   How does the circumcision transgress the law?

²⁸ *For he is not a Jew, which is one outwardly; neither is that circumcision, which is outward in the flesh:*
a.   What is a Jew?
b.   What is circumcision?

²⁹*But he is a Jew, which is one inwardly; and circumcision is that of the heart, in the spirit, and not in the letter; whose praise is not of men, but of God.*
a.   What is an inward Jew?
b.   What is the circumcision of the heart?
c.   How does the spirit differ from the letter?
d.   What does it mean to have praise of God rather than men?

ROMANS – SAMPLE CHAPTER 3

All 21 Strategy of WHAT Study Guides are Available at RomansToJude.com/studyguide

¹*What advantage then hath the Jew? or what profit is there of circumcision?*
a.   What advantage does the Jew have over the Gentile?
b.   How much more profit is there in circumcision than in uncircumcision?

²*Much every way: chiefly, because that unto them were committed the oracles of God.*
a.   What are the oracles of God?
b.   Who are the oracles of God committed to?

³*For what if some did not believe? shall their unbelief make the faith of God without effect?*
a.   What is belief?
b.   What is unbelief?

67

c. What is the faith of God?

d. What is the faith of God without effect?

[4] *God forbid: yea, let God be true, but every man a liar; as it is written, That thou mightest be justified in thy sayings, and mightest overcome when thou art judged.*

a. How is God true?

b. How can every man be a liar?

[5] *But if our unrighteousness commend the righteousness of God, what shall we say? Is God unrighteous who taketh vengeance? (I speak as a man)*

a. What is unrighteousness?

b. What is righteousness of God?

c. What is vengeance?

d. Why does the writer say, "*I speak as a man?*"

[6] *God forbid: for then how shall God judge the world?*

a. What is the world?

b. How does God judge?

[7] *For if the truth of God hath more abounded through my lie unto his glory; why yet am I also judged as a sinner?*

a. What is the truth of God?

b. What is glory?

c. What is a sinner?

d. What does it mean to be judged as a sinner?

[8]*And not rather, (as we be slanderously reported, and as some affirm that we say,) Let us do evil, that good may come? Whose damnation is just.*
a. What is evil?
b. What is good?
c. What is damnation?

[9]*What then? are we better than they? No, in no wise: for we have before proved both Jews and Gentiles, that they are all under sin;*
a. What is a Jew?
b. What is a Gentile?
c. What is sin?
d. How can Jew and Gentiles both be under sin?

[10]*As it is written, There is none righteous, no, not one:*
a. What does it mean to be righteous?
b. Why are there none that are righteous?

[11]*There is none that understandeth, there is none that seeketh after God.*
a. What does it mean to understand?
b. Why are there none that understand?
c. What does it mean to seek after God?
d. Why are there none that seeketh after God?

[12]*They are all gone out of the way, they are together become unprofitable; there is none that doeth good, no, not one.*
a. Who are *they*?
b. What does it mean to be *out of the way*?

c. What does it mean to be unprofitable?
d. What is good?
e. Why is there not one that doeth good?

[13] *Their throat is an open sepulchre; with their tongues they have used deceit; the poison of asps is under their lips:*
a. What do throats, tongues and lips have in common?

[14] *Whose mouth is full of cursing and bitterness:*
a. What is cursing?
b. What is bitterness?
c. Whose mouth is full of cursing and bitterness?

[15] *Their feet are swift to shed blood:*
a. Whose feet are swift to shed blood?

[16] *Destruction and misery are in their ways:*
a. What is destruction?
b. What is misery?
c. Destruction and misery are in *whose* ways?

[17] *And the way of peace have they not known:*
a. What is peace?
b. What is the way of peace?
c. Why haven't *they* known the way of peace?

[18] *There is no fear of God before their eyes.*
a. What is fear?
b. What is the fear of God?

¹⁹*Now we know that what things soever the law saith, it saith to them who are under the law: that every mouth may be stopped, and all the world may become guilty before God.*
a.   What is the law?
b.   What does it mean to be *under the law*?
c.   What is the world?
d.   What is guilt?
e.   What is being guilty before God?

²⁰*Therefore by the deeds of the law there shall no flesh be justified in his sight: for by the law is the knowledge of sin.*
a.   What are deeds of the law?
b.   What is flesh?
c.   What does it mean to be justified?
d.   What is sin?
e.   What is the knowledge of sin?
f.   How is the knowledge of sin *by* the law?

²¹*But now the righteousness of God without the law is manifested, being witnessed by the law and the prophets;*
a.   What does *but now* signify?
b.   What is the righteousness of God?
c.   What is the righteousness of God *without the law*?

²²*Even the righteousness of God which is by faith of Jesus Christ unto all and upon all them that believe: for there is no difference:*
a.   What is the righteousness of God?
b.   What is faith?
c.   What is the faith of Jesus Christ?

d. How is the righteousness of God *by* the faith of Jesus Christ?
e. What does it mean to believe?
f. Is the righteousness of God unto all?

²³*For all have sinned, and come short of the glory of God;*

a. What is sin?
b. Who has sinned?
c. What is the glory of God?
d. What does it mean to *come short* of the glory of God?

²⁴*Being justified freely by his grace through the redemption that is in Christ Jesus:*

a. What is being *justified*?
b. What is *his* grace?
c. What is redemption?
d. How does grace work *through* the redemption that is *in* Jesus Christ?

²⁵*Whom God hath set forth to be a propitiation through faith in his blood, to declare his righteousness for the remission of sins that are past, through the forbearance of God;*

a. What is a propitiation?
b. Who has God set forth to be a propitiation?
c. What is faith?
d. What is *his* blood?
e. How does propitiation come *through* faith in his blood?
f. What is righteousness?
g. What is sin?
h. What is the remission of sins past?

i.   What is the forbearance of God?

²⁶*To declare, I say, at this time his righteousness: that he might be just, and the justifier of him which believeth in Jesus.*
a.   What is *his* righteousness?
b.   What/Who is Jesus?
c.   What is *belief* in Jesus?
d.   What is justification?
e.   Why is one justified for believing in Jesus?

²⁷*Where is boasting then? It is excluded. By what law? of works? Nay: but by the law of faith.*
a.   What is boasting?
b.   What does one have to boast in if God does the justifying?
c.   What are works?
d.   What is the law of faith?
e.   How is boasting excluded by the law of faith?

²⁸*Therefore we conclude that a man is justified by faith without the deeds of the law.*
a.   What is faith?
b.   What is justification?
c.   What does it mean to be justified by faith?
d.   What are deeds?
e.   What is the law?
f.   What are the deeds of the law?

²⁹*Is he the God of the Jews only? is he not also of the Gentiles? Yes, of the Gentiles also:*

a. What is a God of a Jew?
b. What is a God of a Gentile?

[30] *Seeing it is one God, which shall justify the circumcision by faith, and uncircumcision through faith.*

a. What does it mean to be justified *by* faith?
b. What does it mean to be justified *through* faith?
c. Who are the circumcision?
d. Who are the uncircumcision?

[31] *Do we then make void the law through faith? God forbid: yea, we establish the law.*

a. Unto who is the law established if not voided *through* faith?

Resources

Figure 1A: Author's Text Markings of Ephesians

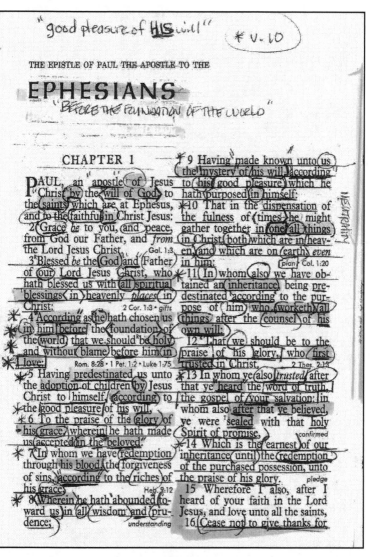

Figure 1B: Author's Text Markings of Ephesians (continued)

His Power Toward us

He Hath Quickened 1723 *Flesh & Mind* + GRACE SAVED - EPHESIANS 2

you, making mention of you in my prayers;

17 That the God of our Lord Jesus Christ, the Father of glory, may give unto you the spirit of wisdom and revelation in the knowledge of him: John 20:17; Col. 1:9

18 The eyes of your understanding being enlightened; that ye may know what is the hope of his calling, and what the riches of the glory of his inheritance in the saints, Acts 26:18 • heart • illuminated

19 And what is the exceeding greatness of his power to us-ward who believe, according to the working of his mighty power,

20 Which he wrought in Christ, when he raised him from the dead, and set him at his own right hand in the heavenly places,

21 Far above all principality, and power, and might, and dominion, and every name that is named, not only in this world, but also in that which is to come: Rom. 8:38

22 And hath put all things under his feet, and gave him to be the head over all things to the church,

23 Which is his body, the fulness of him that filleth all in all.

CHAPTER 2

AND you hath he quickened, who were dead in trespasses and sins; *gave life*

2 Wherein in time past ye walked according to the course of this world, according to the prince of the power of the air, the spirit that now worketh in the children of disobedience: Col. 1:21

3 Among whom also we all had our conversation in times past in the lusts of our flesh, fulfilling the desires of the flesh and of the mind; and were by nature the children of wrath, even as others.

4 But God, who is rich in mercy, for his great love wherewith he loved us, Rom. 10:12 • with which

5 Even when we were dead in sins, hath quickened us together with Christ, (by grace ye are saved;) *made us alive • by whose grace*

6 And hath raised us up together, and made us sit together in heavenly places in Christ Jesus:

7 That in the ages to come he might shew the exceeding riches of his grace in his kindness toward us through Christ Jesus.

8 For by grace are ye saved through faith; and that not of yourselves: it is the gift of God:

9 Not of works, lest any man should boast. *effort • glory*

10 For we are his workmanship, created in Christ Jesus unto good works, which God hath before ordained that we should walk in them. Is. 19:25; Tit. 2:14 • prepared

11 Wherefore remember, that ye being in time past Gentiles in the flesh, who are called Uncircumcision by that which is called the Circumcision in the flesh made by hands; Rom. 2:28, 29; 1 Cor. 12:2; Col. 2:11

12 That at that time ye were without Christ, being aliens from the commonwealth of Israel, and strangers from the covenants of promise, having no hope, and without God in the world:

Acknowledgments

For your considerable share in the making of this book, I would like to express my deep gratitude to all of you, my co-creators:

UCLA	Tavis Smiley	Thomas Sowell, Ph.D
Caroline Streeter, Ph.D	The Izu Family	John Randolph Price
Charles Stanish, Ph.D	Patti Foster	Louise L. Hay
Tritia Toyota, Ph.D	Reginald E. Johnson	Sheridan McDaniel
Brian Walker, Ph.D	Keith Joseph Wiley	TBN Network
Kristine M. Smith	Israel Houghton	W.E.B. DuBois
Angela Clark	Fred Hammond	Ernest Holmes
Daniel Barrozo	Esther and Jerry Hicks	Albert Pike
Merilee Kern	Eckart Tolle	Max Weber
Ralph Dawson, Ph.D	Tracy R. Twyman	King James
Wendy R. Gladney	Wayne Dyer, Ph.D	Lao Tzu

Mom, Olga, Gary, Cynthia, Kamari and Ryan – Thank you.

All of my friends who read this offering as a favor to me – Thank you.

"I pray you, then receive my little book in all charity, studying my words with me, forgiving mistake and foible for sake of the faith and passion that is in me, and seeking the grain of truth hidden there."

- **W.E.B. Dubois**

About the Author

$\mathcal{C}$handel L. White is the author of Romans to Jude – Precise Christian Scripture Revealed – a fresh and insightful "how to" reading strategy guide that helps truth-seekers accurately interpret and better understand the New Testament.

White has been interested in humanity's relationship with the ethereal and textual truth of God since early childhood. These curiosities have lead him on a 30-year journey filled with enlightened experiences with various spiritual organizations: Christian (denominational and non-denominational), Mormon, Jehovah's Witnesses, The Nation of Islam, and Science of Mind. In addition, he has also followed the teachings of many of America's most well known Christian leaders as well as philosophies and works by John Randolph Price, Louise L. Hay, Eckhart Tolle, Ernest Holmes, Wayne Dyer, Esther Hicks, Robert Lomas, Thomas Sowell Ph.D, W.E.B. DuBois, Albert Pike and Max Weber. White has also developed a great appreciation for the insight of the Bhagavad-Gita, the Tao Te Ching and the philosophy of Zen.

With a holistic approach to religion and a passion for teaching fellow Christians, White's book Romans to Jude – Precise Christian Scripture Revealed is helping individuals world-wide accurately read, interpret and apply scripture to their lives with an exact perception of Biblical truth, just as the original writers intended. White seeks to help as many Christians as possible discover the unadulterated truth about Jesus Christ and the mystery of his coming.

White, a father of two, holds an undergraduate degree in Cultural Anthropology from the University of California, Los Angeles.

Contact the Author

Publisher:	Del Aaronson Publishing
Public Relations:	PR@RomansToJude.com
Book the Author:	info@RomansToJude.com
Author's Website:	RomansToJude.com
Author's Email:	author@RomansToJude.com
eBook Orders:	To order eBook edtions of the Strategy of WHAT Study Guides, please visit us at:

RomansToJude.com/studyguide

Available Study Guides:

Romans	Titus
I Corinthians	Philemon
II Corinthians	Hebrews
Galatians	James
Ephesians	I Peter
Philippians	II Peter
Colossians	I John
I Thessalonians	II John
II Thessalonians	III John
I Timothy	Jude
II Timothy	

Index

Made in the USA
Charleston, SC
04 November 2011